Danes

IN WISCONSIN

Revised and Expanded Edition

Frederick Hale

THE WISCONSIN HISTORICAL SOCIETY PRESS

Madison

Published by the Wisconsin Historical Society Press

© 2005 by The State Historical Society of Wisconsin

Photographs identified with PH, WHi, or WHS are from the Society's collections; address inquiries about such photos to the Visual Materials Archivist at the above address.

Publications of the Wisconsin Historical Society are available at quantity discounts for promotions, fund raising, and educational use. Write to the above address for more information.

Printed in the United States of America
Text and cover designed by Jane Tenenbaum

09 08 07 06 05   5 4 3 2 1

Library of Congress Cataloging-in-Publication Data
available

⊗ The paper used in this publication meets the minimum requirements of the American National Standard for Information Sciences-Permanence of Paper for Printed Library Materials, ANSI Z39.48-1992.

Wisconsin's Danish-Born Population c. 1890

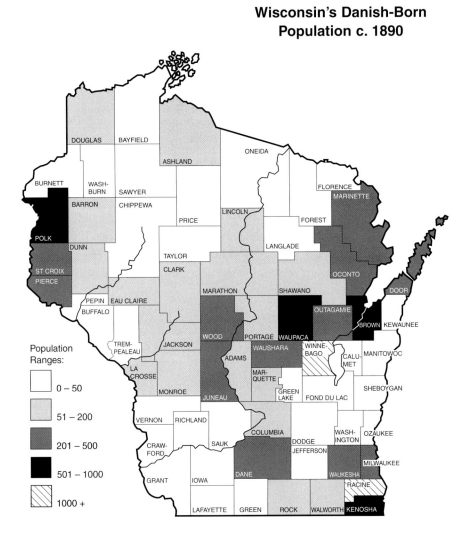

Population Ranges:

- 0 – 50
- 51 – 200
- 201 – 500
- 501 – 1000
- 1000 +

Map by Joel Heiman

WISCONSIN'S FIRST DANES

In 1843 Laurits Jacob Fribert, a young lawyer from Copenhagen, left a promising career in his homeland to become a farmer in Waukesha County, Wisconsin. He was not the first Dane in the territory; Charles Borup, who ran a trading post in the Apostle Islands from 1829 until 1848, probably merits that distinction. An otherwise anonymous hunter with the obviously Americanized name John Smith who reportedly roamed Wisconsin Territory's forests in the mid-1830s and later lived in Polk County may have been the second. John Bang, a builder who settled in Racine at the end of that decade, was probably the first to leave any permanent evidence of himself in the southeastern corner of the state, which became a Danish stronghold.

But Laurits Jacob Fribert became far better known. Settling in the small Swedish immigrant colony near Pine Lake, he built a house and arduously cleared one hundred acres of land. After a few years this newcomer to the agrarian life resumed his former profession in a law firm in Watertown. Before doing so, however, he wrote the first Danish immigrant book about the United States. Published in Norway in 1847, a year before Wisconsin attained statehood, Fribert's *Haandbog for Emigranter til Amerikas Vest* (Manual for Emigrants to the American West) enthusiastically described the region now known as the Upper Midwest as a haven for impoverished Scandinavians in search of land. In contrast to the southern states, he assured concerned readers, it was not overrun with Negro slaves, alligators, poisonous snakes, and other hostile elements. Moreover, its climate was more amenable to Scandinavians than was that of Dixie. Fribert also compared the region favorably to the eastern seaboard, where land was prohibitively expensive. In the West, he wrote, "land costs only $1.25 per acre, requires plowing only once and no fertilizer, and often yields as much the first year as soil that has been cultivated for a long time."

Of the suitable states and territories, Fribert was most favorably dis-posed to his adopted "Viskonsin" because of its supposedly more fertile soil and healthier climate. In addition, Norwegian and Swedish settle-ments had already begun to dot part of the territory—encouraging words to prospective Nordic immigrants. Fribert denied that Wisconsin was swarming with wild Indians and other "false rumors" then current in Scandinavia. Assuring his readers that employment was available and land could be readily purchased or claimed, he declared succinctly: "Everyone should come to Wisconsin!"

Indeed, several dozen of his fellow Danes had already done so. Some of the counties bordering Lake Michigan were beginning to show the first signs of becoming the eastern end of a loose "Danish belt" that eventu-ally extended from them and Chicago through Wisconsin, across Iowa and southern Minnesota, and into eastern Nebraska and South Dakota. Racine County, which by the 1890s was among the most heavily Danish regions of the United States, boasted a tiny flock of Danes whom Frib-ert described. Among them was an agriculturalist named Peter Lutkin who entered the state legislature in 1857, one of the first Scandinavians in the country to be elected to public office.

From Racine, Danes had gradually spread northward and westward. One of the first decidedly Danish settlements was Hartland in Waukesha County, founded in 1846. Another, appropriately called New Denmark (now simply Denmark), followed in Brown County in 1848. Those ham-lets were the nuclei of what developed into one of the most important re-gions of Danish immigration in the United States. In addition to them, some early Danes, like Fribert, settled in or near Norwegian or Swedish communities. Claus Laurids Clausen, for instance, a native of the Dan-ish island of Aero, became at age twenty-three the first pastor of the Nor-wegian settlement at Muskego in Racine County. In the 1840s Kenosha County also attracted Danes, although they did not form a distinctive ethnic community at the time.

Little is known about most of the Danes who emigrated to Wiscon-sin before midcentury, but many, like Fribert, seem to have been adven-turesome individuals who had not occupied the lowest rungs of the social ladder in their homeland. Some were probably compelled less by eco-nomic pressures than by the challenge of a new lifestyle to leave the rel-ative security of Denmark for the hardships of frontier Wisconsin.

As time passed, however, the ability of the Danish economy to support a rapidly growing population showed signs of strain and gave many Danes abundant reasons to leave. Medical care made great strides in Scandinavia during the nineteenth century, and the rate of infant mortality dropped markedly. Owing partly to this, Denmark's population leaped from approximately nine hundred thousand in 1800 to over 2.8 million by the outbreak of World War I in 1914. This growth reflected the trend in most other European countries. As was the case in Germany, Poland, and many other lands, Denmark, with roughly 43,000 square kilometers (Wisconsin, for purposes of comparison, has about 146,000 square kilometers), simply did not have enough territory to distribute among its people.

The rural areas felt the pinch first. Denmark remained a predominately agrarian society for much of the nineteenth century, one that had both a limited number of wealthy owners of estates and countless smallholders (*gårdejere*) but a far greater number of landless peasants (*tyende*) who labored as farmhands in the fields of their more fortunate countrymen. These rural folk were spread across regions of widely varying fertility. Must of central Jutland, for example, was highly productive. Not surprisingly, that area yielded few emigrants. By contrast, the sandy island of Langeland in southern Denmark lost nearly 20 percent of its population to the New World between 1870 and 1900. The island of Bornholm, a rocky Baltic outpost far to the east of the rest of Denmark, gave up almost 14 percent of its inhabitants during that period. On the other hand, the fertile counties of Zealand north and west of Copenhagen contributed relatively few Danes to America. Land reforms came slowly to Denmark, whose age of absolutism lasted until the kingdom received its first constitution in 1849. But even if the agricultural regions had been evenly distributed among the population, its rapid growth would have quickly pared the plots to a size incapable of supporting families. Indeed, precisely that happened in some areas. But the larger problem was the ever-expanding army of landless peasants unable to find work on their neighbors' holdings.

The Danish cities offered hope to some. During the second half of the nineteenth century the industrial revolution reached Scandinavia. Steam power, the burgeoning of international trade, and other factors stimulated manufacturing and produced an urban working class. Indigent peasants followed their visions of ready employment to the cities, swelling the population of Copenhagen, for instance, from approximately two hundred thousand in 1870 to nearly half a million three decades later. Ålborg and Århus, the two most important cities in Jutland, both tripled in size between 1860 and 1900. To many of the migrants from the countryside, though, the dream of a share in Denmark's growing industrial prosperity proved to be nothing more than an empty pot beneath a monotone rainbow of factories already surrounded by masses of unemployed laborers eager to work. For thousands of Danes, therefore, the cities served only as inhospitable roadhouses on an odyssey that ended in North America.

By the late 1840s, some keen-eyed Danish reformers foresaw these developments and began to encourage their impoverished countrymen to emigrate directly from rural Denmark to the United States. No Dane played a greater role in this effort that Rasmus Sørensen (1799–1865), a farmer's son from Jelling, a village near Vejle in southeastern Jutland. During the 1840s this teacher and lay preacher gained prominence as a defender of the farming class. In his periodical, *Almuevennen* (The Friend of the Peasantry), he advocated tax reductions, schools for farmers, and other causes intended to improve the plight of the rural poor. Progress came slowly, however, and Sørensen considered joining his oldest son, Martin, who had emigrated to the United States in 1844 and was studying at an Episcopal theological seminary in Nashotah, Wisconsin.

When Fribert's book appeared in 1847 it heightened Sørensen's interest in the territory. Since it was published in Norway, Sørensen felt obligated to propagate among the Danes Fribert's gospel of Wisconsin as a near-paradise for Nordic immigrants. The same year, therefore, he wrote a sixteen-page synopsis of the book, cumbersomely titled *Om de udvandrede Nordmaends Tilstand I Nordamerika, og hvor det vilde vaere gavnlig, om endeel danske Bønder og Haandvaerkere udvandrede ligeledes, og bosatte sig sammested* (On the Norwegian Emigrants' Condition in North America, and Why It Would Be Advantageous if Some Danish Farmers and Artisans Likewise Emigrated and Settled in the Same Place).

Declaring that letters from his son had confirmed Fribert's roseate description of Wisconsin, Sørensen enthusiastically portrayed the territory as a veritable Eden free of the burdens that he had campaigned to remove from the shoulders of the Danish poor. The residents of Wisconsin "have practically no taxes or fees," he promised; "they do not pay a tithe to any church, pastor, religious organization, or king." Moreover, stated this advocate of peasant schools, "that which is paid little attention in Denmark, namely education and learning for the farming class," flour-ished in Wisconsin, where "the farmer often goes to school and is taught along with his sons." Unemployment could be left behind in the Old World; in America farmhands could readily earn a dollar a day and re-ceive adequate meals as well. Within "a very short time" they could save enough money to purchase a farm as well as livestock and build a house. Finally, in contrast to the fairly rigid social order of Denmark, "the rela-tionship between landowner and servant is as free and open as possible" in Wisconsin.

The efforts of Sørensen and Fribert to stimulate emigration to Wis-consin soon bore fruit. The number of Danish pioneers in the state rose modestly in the late 1840s. The census of 1850 reported 146 Danish-born residents in Wisconsin, ranking it behind only New York, Massachusetts, and Louisiana, states with important ports of entry for immigrants and burgeoning maritime interests, which even at that early date employed growing numbers of Scandinavian sailors. Significantly, the new state had already attracted more Danes than any of its neighbors—Illinois, Michi-gan, Iowa, and the Territory of Minnesota—although the last two even-tually surpassed it. By midcentury the dual urban and rural lineaments of the Danish American pattern of settlement were thus beginning to emerge. In frontier Wisconsin, however, nearly all of the Danes neces-sarily lived on farms and in villages at that time, although Racine became one of the most important Danish centers in North America during the 1880s.

Delayed by the revolution of 1848, which brought democracy to Denmark, Sørensen did not arrive with his first party of immigrants until 1852. He remained for nine years, farming in Dodge County near Aship-pun and serving as a lay reader in the Episcopal church of which his son was minister. (The church had been started by Swedish immigrant Gustaf Unonius as an offshoot of his nearby church at Pink Lake, a pioneer Swedish settlement.) After a brief visit to his homeland in 1861, Sørensen returned to Wisconsin with 150 additional immigrants, most of whom settled in Waupaca County, then a northern outpost of Danish civiliza-tion in America. The following year, he accompanied an even larger party to Wisconsin.

In the meantime, the Danish-born population of Wisconsin had climbed to 1,150 in 1860. These newcomers were only a small segment of the state's increasingly complex cultural mosaic, however, which by then included 276,927 immigrants, nearly half of whom had come from the lands of the German Confederation. (On the other hand, in 1860 the Danes outnumbered the Swedes and the Poles combined, two groups that made a noticeable impact on the history of Wisconsin.)

THE DIFFICULT JOURNEY

Danes who emigrated to North America before the transition from sail to steam power in the 1860s and 1870s subjected themselves to a trying and occasionally dangerous ocean voyage that typically lasted six weeks and sometimes as long as eight or ten. Since there were no transatlantic passenger vessels under the Danish flag until the 1870s, emigrants had to book passage on foreign ships, usually those of either German or British lines whose agents in Copenhagen and other cities competed vigorously for passengers. Several routes were available, none especially convenient. During the early years of emigration, it was simplest to travel by rail south to either Hamburg or Bremen and join the swarms fleeing the oppressive poverty of central Europe. When the number of emigrating Danes began to rise in the 1870s and 1880s, however, they attracted increasing attention from British lines. It became more common to take a ship across the North Sea to Hull or Newcastle, travel by train across northern England, and board a transatlantic liner in Liverpool. Most sailed to New York, although some Danes entered North America at Quebec, Boston, New Orleans, and other ports.

Seasickness was common. One twenty-two-year-old Dane who sailed with his brother from Hamburg to New York in 1847 and settled in Brown County two years later wrote succinctly to his parents: "It was unpleasant. I didn't have any pain, but since I could hardly eat I began to look rather gaunt." He recovered, but no doubt the two brothers were pleased to spot the American shore after sixty days at sea. Rasmus Sørensen described conditions below decks on his 1852 voyage in vivid terms: "It looked miserable and foul with vomiting, filth, stench, and suffering people, some of whom lay half dead in their berths or on the floor, amid sprawling chests, overturned chamberpots, and full food dishes, without being able to remove the surrounding mess that did not exactly have the odor of roses."

Conflicts between passengers added to the misery. Immigrant ships generally carried passengers from several countries, and under the pressure of long, uncomfortable voyages international rivalries often erupted. Almost invariably forming a small minority on foreign vessels, the Danes had to steer a diplomatic course between mutually hostile camps. A brief war between Denmark and the German Confederation in 1848 and the Austro-Prussian invasion of 1864 honed Danish nationalism, though, and Danes occasionally entered into shipboard frays with German-speaking emigrants.

No less demoralizing were the dishonesty and debauchery of some passengers. "Steerage became a regular brothel," wrote a young Dane from Zealand who sailed to New York in 1851. "People gambled away their clothing and fistfights ensued. We had four prostitutes and at least five thieves. When one of the latter was searched, it was discovered that he had stolen thirty-one different items, including one of my handkerchiefs." Those who could afford private cabins were isolated from much of this misery, but most Danish emigrants had to be content with a rough-and-tumble crossing in steerage.

For those destined for Wisconsin before the Civil War, the Atlantic voyage was the most demanding leg of their journey. There were several routes west from the eastern port of entry. The well-heeled could avail themselves of a journey by rail that brought them via Chicago to the Midwest in a few days. Most, however, pieced together a combination of trains and steamers on the Great Lakes to Milwaukee, a slower route for which Sørensen paid seven dollars in 1852.

ON WISCONSIN SOIL

Land was indeed abundant in Wisconsin, and it could be procured in several ways. Outright purchase of public domain at $1.25 per acre was the simplest, and many immigrants worked as farmhands or at other jobs until they had saved enough to buy small farms that way. Others, however, took advantage of a provision that allowed them to claim 160 acres of federal land and pay for it at the end of the year. The Mexican War (1846–1848) ironically provided a third route to property ownership. To recruit soldiers, the administration of President James K. Polk offered "land warrants," meaning vouchers that could be exchanged for quarter sections of land after the completion of active service. Some veterans had little interest in farming and therefore sold their warrants on the open market, where speculation in them was rife. At times they could be purchased for as little as $100 (about sixty-two cents an acre). The most expensive way of obtaining a farm was simply to buy one privately. The Homestead Act of 1862 played a very limited role for the Danes of eastern Wisconsin, where most of the suitable land was already in private hands by that date.

Preparing an acreage for cultivation was an arduous task. Unforested areas were frequently burned over to remove the tangle of high prairie grass, a practice that fascinated many a Dane. One enterprising immigrant in New Denmark paid $12.50 an acre to have part of his wooded farm cleared and fenced, thereby multiplying his initial investment in it by several times. This Danish bachelor built a small house for himself in a matter of weeks, however, and frequently assured his family in Denmark that economic conditions in Wisconsin were allowing him to expand his holdings.

But nowhere did he or other Danish Americans confirm Fribert's exaggeration that pioneers needed to work only three days a week to develop prosperous farmsteads. Many newly arrived farmhands complained about exploitation by their employers, while others conceded that transforming forests into productive fields was a demanding job that almost invariably took several years. Countless trees had to be felled, and stubborn stumps were often allowed to stand until they rotted away a decade later. In the meantime, farmers weaved their plows between them or allowed small herds of cattle or other livestock to graze in the cutover areas. On the other hand, Lars Jørgenson, an itinerant Baptist missionary who wrote a detailed description of Danish immigrant life in the 1850s and 1860s, pointed out that in some respects conditions were less trying in Wisconsin than in Denmark. "Farm work is not strenuous, except for a week in the spring and autumn," he promised. To bolster his assertion, Jørgenson noted that fencing was "an easy chore" owing to the abundance of usable logs, music to the ears of Danes accustomed to building walls with stones or by painstakingly piecing together small branches in basketweave patterns. Moreover, he stated, "ditches are seldom dug here, and peat is never cut."

Employment in nonagricultural trades also looked promising before the Civil War, although a recession in the late 1850s cost some immigrants their jobs. Unskilled Danes sailed the Great Lakes on steamers, toiled in the harbors of Milwaukee and other ports, and drove spikes along Wisconsin's rapidly expanding railways. Wages were modest, typically $100–$200 annually plus room and board. Artisans, such as carpenters, smiths, and wheelwrights, consistently earned more, while girls working as domestic servants were seldom paid more than a scant five dollars a month plus room and board in those early days.

Danes who settled in rural areas during the 1840s and 1850s initially lived in spartan dwellings that quickly dispelled whatever romantic illusions they may have entertained about life on the frontier. "When we reached our goal, we moved into a wretched little hut that a neighbor had placed at our disposal," recalled Johan Mathiesen, a native of the island of Langeland whose family emigrated to New Denmark in 1855. "It was a one-room clapboard shack. The floor served as our bed, and when it rained the water ran unhindered through the porous roof." Lack of time and money generally forced Danes in rural Wisconsin to follow the common frontier practice of first building a log cabin with one or two rooms and replacing it with a two-story frame house when circumstances allowed. Building homes of wood was unfamiliar to immigrants from timber-poor Denmark, but in a way it symbolized their new freedom and independence. To Rasmus Sørensen, the greatest difference between the old country and the new was that "the man in his log cabin in his own king and master, and the forest in which he chops wood is his alone."

ADAPTATION AND CHANGE

Since the Danes were but a tiny minority in antebellum Wisconsin, their relations with other groups, especially indigenous Americans, were crucial to their adaptation. A few settled in areas with Danish majorities. Mathiesen, for example, recalled that in the 1850s all of his family's neighbors in the New Denmark vicinity were Danes. More typically, however, even immigrants who settled in rural districts were exposed almost daily to "Yankees." Rasmus Sørensen explicitly advised prospective Danish Americans not to pay for the luxury of buying land in regions where many of their countrymen had already purchased farms. To the entreprenuring Andreas Frederiksen, who sold his farm near New Denmark after acquiring a larger acerage in Winnebago County in 1861, such counsel may have seemed extraneous. Writing to his family in Denmark on the eve of his move, he noted cryptically, "Here all of our neighbors are Danes, but out there most will be Americans, and I prefer them."

Frederiksen did not explain why Americans made better neighbors, but like many other Danes he frequently praised Yankee ingenuity and technical advances. Denmark took great strides toward modernization during the nineteenth century but nevertheless lagged behind much of the United States. To those raised in Danish villages, the contrasts were striking. Frederiksen, for instance, was certain that Danish blacksmiths should emulate their American counterparts in sprinkling borax on cast iron to increase its malleability. In a similar vein the missionary Lars Jørgensen described how forty-five thousand of the pigs that annually went to market in Milwaukee were slaughtered in one mass-production packing plant: "The animals are herded into a passage so narrow that only one can go through at a time. When one reaches the machine, its head is suddenly sheared off by a pair of knives that form scissors. They cut through its neck simultaneously from above and below. The head falls through an opening, while the carcass is caught by a hooked wheel that dips it into a hot steam bath and removes its hair. The scalded animal, dead and decapitated, is then thrown to the butcher, who completes the procedure."

Railroad construction also fascinated many an early immigrant, as did the telegraph, the widespread use of steam power, and the use of machines by cobblers, tailors, and other craftsmen. To peasants who had sailed across the Atlantic in search of economic opportunity, American methods seemed to offer a ladder of upward social mobility.

Equally impressive to Danes who emigrated either before or shortly after their native land began its experiment in constitutional democracy in 1849 was the seeming equality of Americans. Their letters teemed with praise of social egalitarianism on the Wisconsin frontier. "The peasantry, bourgeoisie, and officials are all respected alike," reported Jørgensen in the early 1860s. Sørensen echoed this sentiment and wrote (to the probable surprise of readers in Denmark) that even the most prosperous farmers in Wisconsin toiled alongside their hired men in the fields and forests. Such perceptions often prompted early Danish immigrants to accept uncritically the American myth of virtually unlimited opportunity in the

New World. Jørgensen spoke for many in declaring that "in America . . . anyone can become a general, a governor, or even president, provided he has the intelligence and ability." European immigrants had a share of American prosperity, he insisted: "Within a few years they turn uninhabited deserts into productive, cultivated land and build roads, towns, factories, mills, schools, and so on."

This land of supposedly boundless freedom nurtured Yankee ambitions that the Danes found enviable. Penniless "Americans," as Scandinavian newcomers unfailingly called those who, in contrast to themselves, had been born in the United States of American parentage, had come to Wisconsin by the thousands and acquired farms that they sold at a considerable profit a few years later before moving farther west, observed Sørensen. Immigrants from several countries, he noted, had caught this speculative fever and frequently followed in the Yankees' footsteps to Minnesota, Iowa, and other states and territories to the west.

Partly because Danes were numerically weak in Wisconsin before the Civil War, they appear to have assimilated American ways rapidly. Learning English was a crucial part of most newcomers' adaptation, and those from Denmark were no exception. Scandinavian periodicals were published in Wisconsin and other states during the 1850s, but most were oriented chiefly toward a Norwegian or Swedish readership. Adult Danes were thus compelled to read the Norwegian immigrant newspapers—no great task, since that language was nearly identical to their own in its written form at that time—or else learn English. "For us older folks," lamented Sørensen at age fifty-six, "trying to speak English is about like breaking through a wall." His consolation was that "all of the children learn it with the most amazing speed."

Andreas Frederiksen, who favored rapid assimilation, wondered whether it was worthwhile to teach his children Danish. Instead, his oldest daughter began to acquire American social graces by taking piano lessons. Many Danish surnames were Anglicized, or partly so. Sørensen invariably became Sorensen or Sorenson. Many a Nielsen became Nelson, while the newcomer from Langeland, Johan Mathiesen, was redubbed John Matteson. Frederiksen changed his patronymic in steps, proceeding via Frederikson to Frederickson. (Meanwhile, his given name, Andreas, predictably became Andrew.) The second generation seldom bore such well-worn Danish names as Jens, Søren, Carsten, or Birgitte. Surrounded by non-Danes, most of whom spoke either English or German, and having little exposure to Danish ways apart from their parents, the children grew up nearly as Americanized as their schoolmates whose families had migrated from New England or elsewhere in the United States.

One institution that helped many newcomers retain some measure of their cultural identity in North America, the ethnic church, played a very modest role among Danish immigrants before the Civil War. Nearly all had been nominal members of the Lutheran state church in the old country, whose constitution of 1849 had belatedly given some degree of religious toleration while preserving the Lutheran establishment. Yet official membership in it apparently meant little to most. Attendance was weak; the anticlerical rhetoric of Søren Kierkegaard and other critics of the state-church system was strong. No less importantly, the ratio of laymen to the pastors whom the government appointed to guide their spiritual lives widened considerably as Denmark's population grew. In the cities, especially Copenhagen, parishes grew to Brobdingnagian proportions that precluded any sense of cohesion or belonging.

Partly because of these basic demographic factors, Denmark had put one foot into the secular, post-Protestant age by about 1860, more than two decades before emigration from that country crested. The nonchalant religious background of Danish Americans, together with their diffused settlement pattern in the New World, helps to explain why no specifically Danish Lutheran churches were formed in the United States until after the Civil War. Both Lutherans and other denominations, most notably Baptists and Methodists, gathered mixed Dano-Norwegian congregations in Wisconsin and surrounding states beginning around mid-century. Several of them thrived, but they included only a small fraction of the Danes. Some Danes joined Yankee, Norwegian, or other churches, but many, perhaps most, apparently remained aloof.

THE IMPACT OF WAR

The Civil War marked the end of the first phase of Danish emigration to the United States. Reliable statistics of the annual migration begin only in 1868, but all indications are that the moderate flow of the 1850s became an intermittent trickle, but never stopped, after hostilities erupted in 1861. Those Danes already in Wisconsin initially viewed the conflict as a distant affair that did not concern them directly. Sørensen, still optimistic about the state as a haven for Scandinavians, visited Denmark in 1861 and, assuring his countrymen that Wisconsin was still a feasible place for settlement, accompanied 150 more of them there. The following year he encouraged Danes to come to the Badger State and help fill rural jobs left by Yankee lads who had marched off to war. The Homestead Act of 1862 heightened his optimism. Little suitable land was still unclaimed in Wisconsin, but the law had prompted many Americans to sell their established farms there at bargain prices in order to take quarter sections farther west. As the war dragged on, Sørensen's enthusiasm waned, however, and in 1863 he published in Copenhagen a booklet advising prospective emigrants to consider Canada instead.

Some Wisconsin Danes were exposed to the ferocity of the war. In mid-1862 President Lincoln ordered governors of the Union states to draft men into their militias. The Enrollment Act of March 1863 required most men between the ages of twenty and forty-five to register for conscription. Many Danes complied and, generally lacking the $300 exemption fee, were forced to don the blue woolens of the Union armies. Others, like countless Yankees, refused to participate in the carnage but were seldom prosecuted for evasion. One Danish family gave sons to both sides. J. R. Lund, oldest son of artist Theodore Lund of Racine County, was caught in New Orleans while visiting others in his family and had to serve in the Confederate army. He survived, but his brother Charles was not as lucky and died of disease while serving in an Ohio regiment.

A number of Danes enlisted in the Fifteenth Wisconsin Infantry, a regiment made up of midwestern Scandinavians under command of a Norwegian, Colonel Hans Christian Heg. Heavy action in Kentucky, Tennessee, and Georgia sent nearly one-third of its Nordic troops to their graves. Lars Jørgensen, the Danish Baptist missionary, visited that outfit and several others while serving as chaplain. "All of the horrible scenes I witnessed while staying in hospitals both day and night took their toll on my body and soul," he wrote afterward. "Most heart-rending were the cries of the wounded in the dark and the stillness of night. When oaths and swearing were added to the cries, it was like hell to my ears."

AMERICA FEVER

Scandinavian emigration to the United States surged anew after the fires of that inferno subsided in 1865. Indeed, the mass migration of Nordic peoples to America can be dated from the late 1860s. More than four thousand Danes entered the country in 1869. Four years later the figure approached seven thousand. Reflecting the contours of the American business cycle and the attendant employment outlook, Danish emigration plummeted after the depression of 1873 became known in Europe, but it began to rise sharply five years later. It crested in 1882, when well over eleven thousand Danes left their homeland. The recession of the 1880s caused another decline, followed by a surge in the early 1890s. That decade was one of economic woe, however, and the next major wave did not arrive until shortly after the turn of the century.

Wisconsin remained a favorite destination for these newcomers, even though its chief Danish promoter, Rasmus Sørensen, had died in Denmark a few weeks after the Civil War ended and the Homestead Act made other areas of the country, especially the Great Plains, more attractive than they had been. The number of Danish-born residents of Wisconsin climbed from 1,150 in 1860 to 5,212 a decade later. Most were still in rural districts in 1870; Milwaukee counted only 116 of them in that year. By that time, Wisconsin had more Danes than any other state; Illinois was second with 3,711. At the end of the century, however, Iowa had pulled into the lead with 17,102 Danish-born residents, while Wisconsin with 16,171 ranked third behind Minnesota but slightly ahead of Illinois and Nebraska. These five contiguous states remained the heart of the "Danish belt" until internal migration, especially to California, disrupted the pattern and the flow of northern European immigrants was drastically reduced in the 1920s.

An intricate network of agents and subagents scattered across Denmark whipped up "America fever" during these years of mass emigration. Representing shipping and railway lines, real estate companies, and other concerns with a vested interest in persuading Danes to leave their native land, they flooded the Danish press with a stream of rhetoric proclaiming the supposed glories of the New World. They also sold tickets; if a small-town Dane wanted to move to Wisconsin, he could book passage from his community to Milwaukee in a subagent's office only a

A subsistence farmer's home in Zealand, Denmark, during the 1880s.

Courtesy of ARoS Aarhus Kunstmuseum

Emigrants boarding a ship at Larsen Square in Copenhagen (from Edvard Petersen's painting of 1890).

Danes World Wide Archive

The *Thingvalla* steams out of Copenhagen in the 1890s in this painting by Vilhelm Arnesen.

Old World Wisconsin

The harsh realities of life in the New World were suggested in this view of a Danish farm built by Kristen Pedersen in the Town of Luck, Polk County, in 1872. (The Pedersen house is preserved at the Wisconsin Historical Society's Old World Wisconsin historic site, near Eagle.)

WHS Name File; WHi(X3)46448

Wisconsin Territory's first Dane, Charles William Borup, ran a trading post in the Apostle Islands from 1829 to 1848.

Courtesy of V. Wunsch; WHi(X3)36774

Early Wisconsin Dane John Bang.

WHi(X3)36910

The young Danish pastor Claus L. Clausen ministered to the Norwegian Lutheran congregation in Muskego, Racine County, in the 1840s.

Laurits Jacob Fribert, one of Wisconsin's earliest Danes, settled in Waukesha County in 1843. In his *Haandbog for Emigranter til Amerikas Vest* (Manual
for Emigrants to the American West), published in Norway in 1847, he pro-
claimed, "Everyone should come to Wisconsin!"

Like Fribert, Rasmus Sørensen had a great impact on Danish immigration to Wisconsin. He accompanied large groups of Danes to the state in 1852 and 1861.

Hans Borschsenius, Adjutant with Field and Staff for the Fifteenth Wisconsin Volunteer Infantry. Borschsenius was born in Seeland, Denmark, in 1832 and immigrated to America in 1856, ultimately settling in the town of Christiana. After serving with the Fifteenth Wisconsin, he had careers in politics, law, newspaper publishing, and hospitality. He died in April 1908.

Left: Captain Joseph Mathiesen (also Matheson) of Company B, Fifteenth Wisconsin, was born Joseph Matthiesen in Copenhagen, Denmark, in 1840. He immigrated to America in 1859, just two years before the start of the Civil War. Mathiesen was mustered in on November 16, 1861; he is said to have survived his three-year war service with being sick, wounded, or captured. After the war Mathiesen settled in Madison, married and had three children, and worked in banking. He died in 1925.

Artist Theodore Lund (here in a self-portrait, date un-known) of Racine saw two sons off to the Civil War, one fighting for the Confederate army and one for the Union. Only one survived.

Courtesy of the Dania Society; WHi(X3)36982

Above: Immigrants formed the Dania Society in 1871 to promote music, debate, and the study of Danish, but the club's activities gradually expanded to include other cultural and recreational pastimes. The Society's bowling team sat for this photo about 1900.

Right: Racine's Old Dania Hall as it appeared in 1876. The site was later occupied by the J. I. Case wheel shop.

Courtesy of the Racine Heritage Center

WHi(W61)21259

A school in Denmark (Brown County), Wisconsin, circa 1893. Denmark, originally called New Denmark, was founded in 1848.

Courtesy of Thorvald Hansen; WHi(X3)36875

Danish parsonage and folk school at West Denmark (now Luck), Polk County, 1896. The folk school operated for only one year (1885–1886), and from 1887 to 1892 the buildings served as a theological seminary for the Danish Evangelical Lutheran Church.

stone's throw from his own doorstep. The dishonesty of some agents eventually led to widespread public suspicion and caused many disillusioned neophyte Americans to send warnings to the editors of their hometown newspapers in Denmark.

Several state governments became directly involved in recruiting immigrants, with Wisconsin leading the way. Its state board of immigration, founded shortly after the Civil War, printed large quantities of promotional literature in Copenhagen for distribution in both Denmark and Norway. The economic troubles of the 1870s interrupted the board's vigorous campaign, but it resumed in the 1880s when Scandinavia disgorged record numbers of emigrants.

The Atlantic crossing underwent a profound transition during the 1860s and 1870s. Marathon crossings in wooden sailing vessels were shortened to ten days or less on steamships that crowded the North Atlantic sea routes. Many Danes continued to book passage on British and German vessels, while a far smaller number sailed on ships of United States, Canadian, or other registry. After the Danish flag-carrier Thingvalla Line began operations in the late 1870s, Danes could embark in Copenhagen for North America and thereby avoid many of the unpleasantries that passengers endured on various foreign lines. Competition was fierce everywhere, however, and to slash expenses the shipping companies continued to shoehorn bodies below decks much as they had done a generation before.

International law eventually regulated maritime passenger conditions, but not before many Danes experienced harrowing ordeals on the high seas. Some of their laments had a familiar ring. "The German crew treated us like pigs," wrote a young couple after settling in Waupaca. "But the food they dourly served us was not even suited for swine." Four others who found homes in Adams County in 1871 regretted sailing on the Allan Line to Quebec and advised readers in Denmark not to duplicate their mistake. After disembarking in eastern Canada, they had taken a series of trains across the provinces of Quebec and Ontario as well as through northern Michigan to Wisconsin. But "the Canadian railway is in wretched condition, and as a result there are a lot of accidents," they warned. Besides, "immigrants never get receipts for their baggage, which is frequently lost." The four blamed their woes partly on "agents who use every trick they have to persuade people to travel on their lines."

The cost of transportation across the Atlantic varied no less in the nineteenth century than in our own time. During the years when emigration was at or near its peak, a Dane typically paid from eighty to one hundred crowns for a ticket to the eastern United States. Shipping companies generally granted their agents the freedom to lower individual fares by about 20 percent to compete in a crowded market. Generally speaking, competition pushed ticket prices down during the second half of the century, while real income for employed Danes rose notably. These two factors naturally made emigration far more feasible for an increasing number of people. Nevertheless, passage to America usually represented at least two or three months' wages for rural workers, who earned approximately four hundred crowns annually in the 1880s and usually had very little liquid capital. In order to pay for two bargain-priced tickets in 1886, one middle-aged cabinetmaker from Copenhagen had to sell at a loss his sofa, four chairs, two tables, and other furniture. In many instances, men who emigrated to the New World saved enough money to send prepaid tickets to wives and younger siblings still in Denmark. During the 1880s and 1890s, about 25 percent of those who left via Copenhagen held them.

WISCONSIN'S DANISH SETTLEMENTS

As the number of Danish newcomers in Wisconsin increased, their pattern of settlement gradually broadened to cover several parts of the state. In the 1840s most of the Danes lived in a wide swath extending roughly from Kenosha to Waupaca to just east of Green Bay. Between these two poles, concentrations were evident in Racine, Waukesha, Winnebago, and Brown Counties. Land prices rose rapidly in southeastern Wisconsin, however, and would-be farmers had to look farther north and west. Washington Island off the tip of Door County attracted a moderate number. Considerably more settled among the Norwegians in Dane County (named after a Revolutionary War figure, Nathan Dane of Massachusetts), adding to two settlements there curiously called Brooklyn and Oregon. Poysippi in Waushara County included several Danish families at an early date, as did the western shore of Lake Winnebago from Neenah to Oshkosh. Indeed, Danes often compared the topography of Winnebago County to that of their native land. "The natural setting of

Lake Winnebago is so similar to that of Skanderborg Lake," wrote Rasmus Sørensen, "that I fall into the most amazing admiration just by seeing the most beautiful sections of my mother country enlarged here several times." Others settled near Clinton in Rock County, Shennington in Monroe County, Big Flats in Adams County, and Ashippun in Dodge County. Most of these settlements were small, but by the mid-1880s they dotted much of eastern, southern, and central Wisconsin.

As the frontier moved westward, Danish, or at least partly Danish, villages cropped up near the Minnesota border. The most evident of these, appropriately called West Denmark, was founded in the 1860s in Polk County. It grew steadily, if on a small scale, and by the 1880s had become the most important center for Danes in western Wisconsin. Subsistence farming and hunting gradually gave way to a balanced agricultural economy. A creamery was built in 1886, though the Minneapolis, St. Paul, and Sault St. Marie Railway did not reach the community until the turn of the century.

In the meantime, shipping at the Duluth-Superior harbor had brought apparent, if vulnerable, prosperity to Douglas County—and with it several hundred Danes. Considerably more found employment in the sawmills of Marinette and in rugged lumber camps along the Michigan border. In the early 1890s a visitor from Denmark reported that that town of sawdust streets (as well as Menominie, Michigan, immediately across the Menominee River from Marinette) was home to nearly seven hundred Danes, most of whom seemed quite prosperous. With a Danish church, school, library, and social organization, Marinette temporarily flourished as a center of Danish culture on Wisconsin's northern frontier.

Withee, northwest of Marshfield in Clark County, owed much of its early history to an arrangement between Yankee timber entrepreneurs from Black River Falls and one of the Danish American Lutheran synods. The denomination hoped to create a colony modeled after a successful one it had sponsored in Lincoln County, Minnesota, during the 1880s. In the early 1890s the John S. Owen Lumber Company promised to give the church a site, build a parsonage, and pay the pastor's salary for a year provided that Danish immigrants could be attracted to the area and induced to purchase cutover timber land at prices averaging about ten dollars an acre. The company retained the right to harvest trees for another five years.

Dozens of Danes, most of whom had already settled elsewhere in

Wisconsin or other states, accepted the offer. A. S. Nielsen, a pastor from Chicago, also came to Withee, but the depression of 1893 forced the company to renege on its promises. Later, new management donated several acres of land and sufficient lumber for the parsonage. Depressed prices for agricultural produce in the 1890s compelled most of the colony's farmers to supplement their meager incomes through additional work. Some found it on railway construction gangs, where they earned a dollar a day for toiling sixty hours a week. Others worked in construction trades or sold wood from their farms for three dollars a chord. The roads, some of which were built of logs, were primitive in northern Wisconsin at that time, but immigrant newspapers in Danish kept Withee's residents in touch with Danes in other settlements. Owing to the village's partial isolation, many of its children retained their proficiency in Danish even though they learned English at school. The church reinforced bilingualism by conducting its worship services in Danish for half a century.

By the 1880s the tentacles of the state's railway network linked together most of the regions in which Danes were continuing to settle, making them accessible with relative ease. Several counties had only a handful of Danish immigrants, and in fact most had fewer than three hundred each when the century ended. Nevertheless, few of these newcomers lived in the cultural semi-isolation that had forced their predecessors to assimilate rapidly. It was now more feasible to establish Danish churches, form Danish cultural and social societies, publish newspapers aimed at Danish readers, and do other things along ethnic lines. One result was a determined if at best only moderately successful effort to preserve *danskhed*, or Danishness, through these and other institutions.

PRESERVING DANISH CULTURE

The most fundamental of Danish institutions was the family. During the second half of the century, the structure of Danish emigration changed from generally that of family units to a decided plurality of young bachelors. Closely related to this, the average age of the immigrants dropped steadily as economic conditions became more constricted in Scandinavia. The results were mixed for forming Danish families in America. The number of eligible women rose somewhat along with the general tide of emigration, so bachelors no longer had to turn immediately to Norwegian, German, Yankee, or other circles to find brides. But the number of Danish bachelors rose even faster, thus intensifying the competition. As one forlorn farmer in Jackson County complained in 1876, "Genuine Danish girls are just as scarce as mills here. The few who come get married immediately."

Ethnic churches helped to preserve Danish culture when they began to multiply after the Civil War. In Wisconsin, the number of Baptist and Methodist congregations, many of which included Norwegian members as well, rose slowly, and Seventh-day Adventist churches also began to appear. Most of the Danes were birthright Lutherans, though, and congregations of that heritage became predominant in the late 1860s and 1870s. Lutheranism, a folk religion among the Scandinavians since the Reformation, may have been expected to serve as a unifying bond among Danish immigrants. Yet it proved to separate just as much as it united them. The root of the problem lay in Denmark, where the state church was divided into two hostile factions in the nineteenth century. Followers of Bishop N. F. S. Grundtvig, a prominent theologian, psalmist, educator, and folklorist, advocated a formalistic, high-church brand of Christianity that incorporated elements of nineteenth-century nationalism. At the other extreme of the Lutheran spectrum, pietists sympathetic to the Inner Mission, an organization promoting revivalism and domestic missionary work, emphasized conversion of the individual and abstention from liquor, the theater, and other worldly pleasures and favored simple liturgy. Relations between the two factions were acrimonious in Denmark and did not improve in the United States.

In 1869 the "Committee to Promote the Preaching of the Gospel among the Danes in North America" was organized in Copenhagen to help struggling Lutheran congregations in the New World secure and support pastors. Its task was difficult, since funds and personnel were in short supply on both sides of the Atlantic. Compounding the problem, several of the clergymen sent to the United States were at least semi-Grundtvigian and thus unacceptable in pietistic circles. Nevertheless, congregations in Racine and several other communities constituted at a meeting held in Neenah in 1872 what was later called "The Danish Evangelical Lutheran Church in America." The new denomination emphasized unabashedly that it was "a branch of the Danish national church," *i.e.*, the state church of Denmark. Indeed, it occasionally received modest financial support from the Danish government. Moreover, it continued to rely on the church in Denmark for many of its pastors until 1887, when a small seminary was opened at West Denmark. Accommodated in two wooden frame houses, it enrolled a total of twenty-seven students, eighteen of whom were eventually ordained. Theological squabbles forced it to close after five years. The denomination resumed its program of pastoral education at Grand View College in Des Moines, Iowa, in 1896, two years after a schism had reduced its size. Such theological bickering was conducted mainly in clerical circles, although the Danish-language press paid considerable attention to it. One early Danish American historian who visited Polk County in 1894 found its laypeople uniformly indifferent to the debate and interested only in restoring harmony.

In the meantime, pietistic Danish immigrants had joined with like-minded Norwegians in 1870 to form the Norwegian-Danish Conference. Fourteen years later, shortly after immigration from Scandinavia peaked, the Danes felt strong enough to secede and organize the Danish Evangelical Lutheran Church society. Leaders of the new denomination frequently leveled verbal assaults at their counterparts in the semi-Grundtvigian body formed twelve years earlier, who often returned the favor.

The pietists' newspaper, *Danskeren* (The Dane), which carried both religious and secular news, was published for several years at Neenah, one of the denomination's strongholds. In 1893 a critical journalist from the liberal Copenhagen daily *Politiken* described the church's influence in that area: "Dark pietism and the missionary cause lie upon the Danes in Neenah and Waupaca like a dead hand. . . . The pastor's sermon is the principle influence on them. It captures the most active, those who ought to be the salt of the Danish community, and draws them into ascetic pietism. All of the others, those who cannot take the religious path, wander into the crude life of the saloon."

The number of Danes in Wisconsin whose lives revolved around the saloon is unknown, but in any case the Danish churches attracted relatively few. Thorvald Lyngby, the pastor of one of Racine's several Danish congregations, gave a representative evaluation of the degree of immigrant religious activity in 1882. His own large flock numbered "about 160 registered, contributing members," but that figure was "nothing compared to the number of Danes in Racine." Comparisons of United States census reports and statistics of church membership reveal that fewer than

10 percent of the Danish immigrants in the entire nation affiliated with specifically Danish churches. How many others joined congregations dominated by other ethnic groups is impossible to determine. In any case, secularization had made wide inroads among Danes on both sides of the Atlantic, and the splintering of the spiritually awakened into several denominations ruled out any unity on religious grounds.

Strictly speaking, American Lutherans of Danish ancestry are still divided into two denominations. The quasi-Grundtvigian party, eventually known as the American Evangelical Lutheran Church, joined with other synods of German, Swedish, and Finnish heritage in 1962 to form the Lutheran Church in America. The more pietistic wing, for decades called the United Evangelical Lutheran Church, participated in the merger that brought about the American Lutheran Church in 1961. The issues that long separated Danish American Lutherans have faded, however, and the present denominations enjoy harmonious relations with each other.

The economy of Wisconsin, like that of many other states, changed from a largely agricultural to a mixed agricultural and industrial one during the last decades of the nineteenth century. Denmark was undergoing a similar transition at that time. It was therefore natural for Danish newcomers to find employment in a broadening spectrum of occupations. One field to which they contributed directly was dairying, which had made rapid strides in Denmark. Farmers there had modernized their facilities and begun to market their products cooperatively. Some believed that America could learn from the success of this experiment. Hans B. Hoiberg (originally Højbjerg), for instance, who had learned dairying at several co-ops before emigrating, settled near Brooklyn in southern Dane County in 1888 and worked there during the 1890s at one of the state's few rural creameries. In 1898 he became manager of Oak Hill Creamery, a cooperative based on Danish principles. Six years later, Hoiberg owned his own dairy in Brooklyn and eventually became an officer of the National Buttermakers Association.

Brewing also became a leading industry almost simultaneously in Wisconsin and Denmark, whose renowned Carlsberg and Tuborg breweries in Copenhagen both date from the nineteenth century. Several Danes worked in that trade on both sides of the Atlantic. One group of young men found employment at a brewery in La Crosse in 1892 but complained that their German supervisors discriminated against them. They also noted that the techniques used in the United States differed from those they had been accustomed to in Denmark. The finished product, they wrote in disgust, tasted "heavy and rancid."

Relatively few Nordic immigrants had been employed in manufacturing in their native lands, but many from rural backgrounds nevertheless found jobs in American factories. The J. I. Case farm implement plant in Racine hired many of that city's numerous Danes. Thorvald Lyngby, the Danish pastor, reported in 1882 that 80 percent of the labor force at the Mitchell & Lewis wagon works there were Danes. Others toiled in "a kettle factory where the workers do so much hammering that one can become partially deaf just by walking past on the street." Lyngby had mixed feelings about the prospects for Danes in Racine. "In material respects Racine is far more favorable to the poor man than Denmark," he stated. "It is a fact that a man can work his way up over here." On the other hand, he conceded, "many of our countrymen sink into crudeness, animal lust, and wilfulness."

To assist their fellow immigrants and to preserve Danish culture in Racine, a small group of Danes led by Julius Stahr founded the Dania Society there in 1867. According to its constitution, the society was to promote music, debating, and language study among its members and to support Danes in cases of illness or the death of breadwinners. Dania thus resembled mutual aid societies organized among many immigrant groups, including some among Danes in Chicago and elsewhere. Its cultural activities featured evening courses in English, dramatic and choral groups, the celebration of Danish holidays, and sponsorship of a library that soon boasted twenty-five hundred volumes. Women's auxiliaries provided much of the strength behind the scenes and contributed to a "Ten Cent Society" whose funds were used for beneficent purposes. In 1871 Dania's sixty members built the first modest Dania Hall, which it replaced in 1905 for the princely sum of $35,000. Membership then numbered approximately eight hundred. In 1876 the society incorporated under Wisconsin laws. Six years later, it became the cornerstone of the newly organized United Danish Societies of America. Although for all practical purposes the Danish language died out in America early in the twentieth century, the Dania Society continues to serve a social function among people of Danish ancestry in Racine.

Most immigrant groups in the United States made some effort to impart their ethnic identity to their children, and the Danes were no exception. Unfortunately, their general dispersion militated against this goal in most parts of the country, where they were a numerically insignificant minority. The concentrations in Racine and, to lesser degrees, in Waupaca, Polk, and Winnebago Counties raised hopes that at least in those places the second generation would be bilingual and firmly grounded in both Danish and American culture. In a few communities, ambitious Grundtvigian clergymen sought to achieve this goal by organizing parochial schools that the children would attend on a regular basis instead of the public schools.

Danish language and history formed part of their curricula, as did folk songs in the native language. Since the public schools offered little religious education (other than "nonsectarian" but regular Bible readings in many before the practice became illegal in Wisconsin in 1889), the Danish parochial schools also gave the children a measure of Lutheran catechetical instruction. Racine was naturally one center of this experiment. It enjoyed only modest and temporary success. Qualified teachers were difficult to retain at a monthly salary of twenty-five to thirty dollars, and one was dismissed outright for undisclosed reasons. By the late 1890s the parochial school scheme, which had never developed fully, was on its way out. John H. Bille, a pioneering historian of Danish American life, in 1896 described its results as "insignificant" and estimated that fewer than one thousand children had attended the schools long enough to have been shaped by them.

A related and slightly more successful project was the planting of Danish "folk high schools" in several immigrant communities. In these residential institutions, which traced their origins to Grundtvig in Denmark, youth would spend several months preparing for adult life, learning Danish traditions, and receiving Christian education. One was opened in Polk County in 1884. In an atmosphere of optimism, and motivated by lofty goals, about five hundred people trekked to its lakeside location to hear dedication speeches and to launch the school on its course. It folded after only one year, however, and an effort to revive it in the 1890s was also short-lived. On the whole, the folk high school movement was of little importance in the United States, in contrast to Scandinavia, where it continues to thrive. Bille suggested that not even one second-generation Danish American in a thousand had attended a folk high school and attributed their failure to "the almost total indifference of the Danes, at large, to these schools."

In fact, in Wisconsin and many other states some Danish immigrants were outspokenly opposed to the effort to keep their children linked to the Old World culture of their ancestors. To many, it seemed unrealistic and appeared to threaten the second generation's chances of acceptance and success in what was obviously their native land. P. Sørensen Vig, a clergyman who taught at the seminary in West Denmark, Polk County, opened a debate on the matter in the Danish immigrant press in 1888. "We would indeed serve ourselves and our children poorly by doing everything in our power to prevent them from becoming Americanized," he declared. "To keep the children born in this country from coming into contact with its language and life is a violation of nature that will take its revenge in the long run."

Vig's fears were for naught. The second generation was not prevented from learning American ways or the language with which many of their immigrant parents had struggled. On the contrary, they assimilated rapidly in American society, perhaps more so than the offspring of newcomers from many other lands. This was almost inevitable. Danes were spread thinly throughout much of Wisconsin; in nearly all communities they constituted only a small percentage of the population. Even in Racine, whose Danish American residents frequently boasted it was the most Danish city in the United States, other ethnic groups collectively led by a wide margin. By 1940, when emigration was largely over, the city had approximately twenty-five hundred Danish-born inhabitants, a figure surpassed by combining immigrants from Germany and Czechoslovakia alone, not to mention other groups. (At that time the population of Racine was 67,195.)

Given this basic demographic fact, there was little chance that much cultural identity would be preserved. The flow of Danish immigrants into Wisconsin tapered off sharply after the outbreak of World War I. Without a continuing influx of native speakers, the Danish language began to disappear, a process accelerated by the passing of the first generation and the xenophobic hysteria of the war era. During the "roaring twenties" few second-generation Danish Americans, educated in American schools and usually lacking more than a smattering of their parents' tongue, showed any fervor for cultivating the folkways of their ancestors. Nearly all of the churches where the Gospel had once been preached in Danish had made the transition to English before the Great Depression. Even in the Dania Society of Racine, where many newcomers had been taught the rudiments of Yankee speech, Danish gradually became a curiosity associated with a dwindling number of old-timers. For all intents and purposes the saga of Danish immigration was over.

For several decades before the mid-1920s, when Congress imposed a quota system that drastically reduced immigration, historians of that massive social movement published dozens of books glorifying the accomplishments of their respective ethnic groups. By presenting a one-sided and usually romanticized image of these contributions, they hoped to increase their own generation's chances of being accepted as worthy newcomers who were fully willing to assimilate in the mainstream of middle-class America. There is no need to broadcast a distorted picture of the Danes in Wisconsin, however, and it would be dishonest to magnify their role in the state's history. The number who emigrated to North America as a whole was not great—about 300,000 as opposed to approximately 800,000 Norwegians and roughly 1,200,000 Swedes, to cite the two most relevant comparisons. While Wisconsin attracted more Danish newcomers than most other states, they never constituted more than about 1 percent of the state's population. Nordic in appearance, nominally if hardly fervent Protestant in religious affiliation, politically moderate, geographically dispersed, and economically prosperous, most Danes soon became inconspicuous fibers in the social warp and woof of the Badger State.

WHi(X3)32444

Workers at the J. I. Case Company, 1884. Case employed many Danes at its farm implements factory in Racine.

WHi(X3)35452

Racine, Wisconsin, in 1888, looking northeastward from the courthouse. By the 1890s Racine was the most important Danish center in the United States

Courtesy of Carolyn Heidemann; WHi(X3)36941

Class photo taken at Racine's Fifth Ward School, 1888. The ward was known as "Little Denmark" at that time.

Fair Day in Denmark, Wisconsin, 1910, when area farmers—many of Danish descent—gathered to buy and sell cattle, hogs, ducks, and geese.

Many Danish immigrants arrived in Wisconsin with significant experience in dairying, and the group made a large contribution to the state's dairy industry. Hans B. Hoiberg had worked in several dairy co-ops in Denmark before he immigrated and settled in Brooklyn, Dane County, in 1888.

WHS Library E184 S19 D34 1908

WHS Library E184 S19 D34 1908

By 1904 Hans Hoiberg owned his own dairy in Brooklyn.

WHi(W61)21258

The Peter Andersen family on their farm in Denmark, Wisconsin, 1890.

Courtesy of Carolyn Heidemann; WHi(X3)36946

Three generations of the Andersen family of Racine, photographed about 1895.

Courtesy of Caroline Miller; WHi(X3)37249

Sleigh-riders in Withee, Wisconsin, 1914. The Danish American Lutheran Church helped form a colony at Withee, in Clark County, in the 1880s.

Courtesy of Caroline Miller; WHi(X3)37250

The Soren Andersen farm in Withee, about 1912. Soren Andersen left Denmark for America in 1872 and became a citizen in 1890.

Courtesy of Howard Paulsen; WHi(X3)36929

The Second Lutheran Church at West Denmark (now Luck) was dedicated in 1900 and destroyed by lightning in 1937.

Courtesy of Carol Larsen; WHi(X3)36964

The logging camp of Anton Larsen, near Tomah (Monroe County), about 1910.

The Dania Society's gymnastics team, Racine, 1924.

Players in the Racine Dania Dramatic Club's 1929 production of *Distrikts Fogden*.

WHS Classified File; WHi(X3)50108

Danish folk dance group in Racine, 1936.

Courtesy of Bethania Lutheran Church

As in most Danish Lutheran churches, a sailing ship hangs in the
nave at Racine's Bethania Lutheran Church, reminding parishioners
of Denmark's seafaring heritage.

PH 3639

Left: Andrew Frederickson, date unknown.
Right: Agathe Johanne Frederickson, date unknown.

THE LETTERS OF ANDREW FREDERICKSON,
1847–1888

The letters of Andrew Frederickson, written over a forty-year span, offer a unique perspective on the Americanization of one Dane who made a new life in Wisconsin. Andreas Frederiksen was born in 1825 in Herslev, Denmark, about a day's journey from Copenhagen. He worked as a wheelwright in Denmark until leaving for America with his boyhood friend Casper Hansen in 1847. After landing in New York, Andreas headed for Wisconsin, where he worked briefly in Milwaukee and later on a Great Lakes ship (the Cleveland*) before settling in New Denmark (now Denmark), in Brown County. Throughout the 1840s and 1850s Frederickson contemplated moving, and he occasionally lived in Wilmington, Illinois, although he always returned to his home in New Denmark. In 1854–55 Andreas returned to Denmark to find a Danish wife and to recruit sixteen others to join the colony of New Denmark. Successful on both his missions, he returned to New Denmark with his wife, Agathe Johanne Jensen (originally Jensdatter). (In his letters Andreas referred to her by her middle name.) By the fall of 1856 Andreas, Johanne, and their daughter, Caroline, were living in Wilmington, but the family returned to New Denmark by 1860. It was around this time that Andreas began signing documents as Andrew Frederickson. In*

1863 Andreas (now Andrew) bought a farm in Neenah, where he lived the re-mainder of his life. Johanne died on May 25, 1888; Andrew lived on until April 17, 1900. Andrew wrote home to family in Denmark regularly, but since his par-ents could not read, he addressed some letters to the pastor of the church in Her-slev. He later addressed his letters to his older brother Niels.

The letters printed here are from Niels Peter Stilling's and Anne Lisbeth Olsen's A New Life: Danish Emigration to North America as Described by the Emigrants Themselves in Letters, 1842–1946 *(Aalborg, Denmark: Danes Worldwide Archives in collaboration with the Danish Society for Emi-gration History, 1994). They are used with the permission of Niels Peter Still-ing, Anne Lisbeth Olsen, and the Danes Worldwide Archives, Aalborg, Denmark. The original letters are located in the Søllerød Museum, Copenhagen, Denmark.*

❧❧

New York, October 5, 1847 [p. 40]

. . . We sailed from Hamburg on Saturday, August 7, but it took two days to get out of the Elbe, and first then can you say the journey to America begins. We had southerly winds, that is, head winds. We sailed north around Scotland and Ireland, and this took much longer than through the Channel. We were both seasick again, and I was sickest, although the seasickness itself was not so bad. But when it was over, I got other ail-ments. Right after the seasickness I became bound up [constipated], and though this was not painful, as I ate practically nothing, I became very weak, and this got even worse when about eight days later I had alto-gether too strong an evacuation [diarrhea]. Many others suffered the same ailments, but Casper has hardly been sick at all.

We have had unfavorable winds for most of the journey, but there has been only one bad storm. We arrived here last evening, and at 6 o'clock today we will take the steamboat to Albany. You will no doubt be happy to hear that already on board ship we made arrangements with a man to work for him, but he has to buy land first, so things were not so definite, but today we are more sure of a position. The German company [the shipowner] was commissioned to hire three or four farmhands for a farm near Buffalo, and although there were many men among the emi-grants, I think most were either craftsmen, but only one wheelwright, or members of families who would not be separated. We received the following offer: 1. Free transport to Buffalo, and we were going through there anyway. 2. 12 dollars a month and free board and washing. When they heard I was a wheelwright, they said that if I could fix his farm implements, I would probably be paid 16 to 18 dollars. 3. When we arrive, we are free to accept the conditions or not, but if we don't, we must, of course, pay for the transportation. The contract can be made for as short or as long a time as we want. If we don't like it, then we will continue to Wisconsin as planned. . . .

September 7, 1848 [pp. 23–24, 56–57]

Dear Parents and Brother! —
I have received your letter, Dear Brother, and have learned of your good fortune with much happiness. The only thing that worries me is that our parents have little chance of pulling through now they are alone. . . . You are a farmer now, perhaps I could also manage somewhat better than our father has done. . . .

My current plan, therefore, is to work for some years and earn as much money as possible and then build a house for myself on my land; then I plan to return home to visit you and to marry, that is, if there is a woman brave enough to come with me to America as women here will do nothing at all outside the house and very little inside, and I would be very embarrassed to have to pay my neighbor half a dollar to put up a load of hay for me if I had a healthy wife. Perhaps I shall stay with you for a winter, and if I should have money and happiness enough to get a farm, I may stay home, but that is hardly to be expected as in this country money is much harder to save than to earn. But I have no desire to become a smallholder in Denmark. Therefore, I beg you, dear parents, do not go to a lot of trouble to keep the house for my sake. . . .

I would not absolutely advise anyone to come over here as, of course, I have no way of foreseeing the consequences; but if I should follow the commandment: "Do unto others as you would have them do to you," then I can only say to all young men who have no one to provide for and no one to provide for them: Come over here, the sooner the better, if you can scrape together money for the journey. I did quite well back home, as you know, but if things had been 100 times better than when I left you, I would still choose to emigrate to America every time. I had about 425 *rigsdaler* [old Danish coinage] when I left home. Now, after three years, and much of that time was spent traveling, I have 240 acres . . . of good land and 600 *rigsdaler.* It is, of course, not likely that everyone will be as lucky as I have been in buying land and earning money, but some of the Danes have also bought more cheaply than I. However, I would still warn people against making a too hasty decision to come over here; everything here will be new to them, and it is not so easy to learn anything as long as you don't understand English. . . .

Rasmus Sørensen writes about how hospitable the people are here. I, however, have never heard of any such thing. You have to pay dearly everywhere for whatever you get. I suggest that anyone who comes over here to work for the farmers should go to Racine. Those who want to buy land should go to Green Bay. Milwaukee is a bad place to end up, as government land has already been sold in a radius of 30 to 40 miles, and small wages are paid for work. . . .

Before I received your letter, I always had money in my pocket, as I thought that if you [Andrew's brother] couldn't get anything, and provided our parents were healthy enough to make the trip, you might have thought of coming over here. But now it is no good talking of that anymore. In that case, I would have gone right away and bought land in Wisconsin where at the present it is both good and well located. But the money was a burden in this way and did not pay any interest. Therefore, as soon as I got your letter, I let Mossin put it in the bank as he knows about that. Incidentally, I speak English almost as well as I speak Danish now, so I could have done it myself. . . .

[In my letter] I spoke about another Dane in this year's group of emigrants whom I helped to get a job here on the ship. He is still here, so I have a friend. He is a fine person but finds the English language very difficult to learn. His name is Frederik Lerche, and his father is teacher Lerche in Lille Hallager near Sorø. You might let him know that his son is fine. I learned some time ago that the second mate here on the ship has sailed on the Mississippi River, and since he likes me, I asked him how that was. He told me what I had heard before, that the work on many of the ships is very hard. He says the wages are 25 to 35 dollars a month. I am thinking about going down there and trying my luck this winter. It does not cost very much. . . .

You are probably surprised that I have gone to sea and do not practice my trade, but that is because here I can always be sure to get what I deserve, but on land that can be difficult. Anyway, the wages are higher. . . .

Milwaukee, November 24, 1848 [p. 58]
. . . If I am lucky in what I earn, I will come back home for a visit before
I decide on anything; now I am not as afraid to travel as when I left you.
Now I am getting ready to travel south to the Mississippi River; maybe I
will go on board early tomorrow morning. I like America better and bet-
ter now that the first homesickness is over. . . .

I remained on board the propeller [paddle steamer] Cleveland until
November 9th. . . . When we were paid, I received 84 dollars. I traveled
to Milwaukee to settle my affairs with the Dane where I have my bed
linens and the clothes I did not want to bring with me—and to put my
money in the bank. I talked with Mossin, who knows the directors of the
bank and who had helped me before. He was most willing to help me
again, but he said: I have taken my own money out of the bank, which
pays only 5 percent interest, and used it to buy "Land Warrants," and I
plan to earn 100 percent on these. So that you can understand this, I must
first explain what a Land Warrant is. The soldiers here are not con-
scripted from among the people, as they are in Denmark, and then forced
to go to war or let themselves be fleeced by barbaric sergeants. Here they
hire volunteers. They serve five years and are given board and 8 dollars
a month, but lately the United States has been at war with Mexico, and
thus has needed many more soldiers than usual. In order to get these—
and that was just about the time when Casper and I arrived here—the
government issued bulletins announcing that able-bodied soldiers could
get 7 dollars a month and 160 acres of land anywhere in the United
States where there was unsold land. The soldiers had to serve as long as
the war lasted, and if one fell, his land and remaining pay would go to
his relatives. A peace treaty has been signed this year. Each soldier now
has a certificate which is good for 160 acres of land. Many of the soldiers
did not need this land, but they have the right to sell the certificate to anyone they choose. The government itself will pay 100 dollars for it; but, of
course, private persons can see their advantage in paying more, and there
is now a lot of speculating in Land Warrants, as these certificates are
called.

Last summer, when there were so many immigrants arriving, they
were expensive, as much as 190 dollars; but now the turnover is slow, and
the speculators must, therefore, sell at a low price or leave their money in
them until next spring. Now they can be bought for 118 dollars, and as
land is the safest thing to invest in, I bought two, and Frederik Lerche

bought one. Together with a ship's carpenter from Lolland called Rasmus Rasmussen and a Norwegian called Peder Pedersen, we sailed 75 English miles north of a little town called Manitowoc where there were many Norwegians. Then we walked 18 miles (our mile is only ½ of a Danish mile) to the northwest. Those who accompanied us had claimed land there, and others who emigrated this year, Niels Hansen Godtfredsen, Frederik Hjorth and two Norwegian Andersen brothers, also live there. Their land is together, and next to it there was enough free land. We did not hesitate to take land there; the land around here is some of the best I think I have ever seen.

The land is rolling; there are 8 to 10 inches of topsoil on a layer of sandy clay. It is all wooded land, but the trees are not close together, and most are not big, but in one corner of my land there is a bog where there are hundreds of pine trees. . . . One of the thickest trees is a sugar maple which you are familiar with if you bought Fribert's book, and I have enough trees to make from 200 to 300 pounds of sugar a year. A little river runs through my land, and there is hops on its banks with bigger and fatter buds than I have seen in Denmark. There are wonderful springs bursting from the rock with water as good as I have ever tasted. . . .

The neighbors' wheat has been very good this year, and there is no doubt that this is very fine land. The land is not plowed here the first year after the trees are cut and burned with the leaves as it is so loose you can kick up 5–6 inches of it with your foot; you just sow the seed and harrow it.

The settlement is new, and the road here—even though it is a main road—is still very difficult to travel with a wagon; but that is how it is everywhere here until the land is cultivated. The post office is only a mile from here, and the towns of Green Bay, Twin Rivers and Manitowoc are all within 15–16 miles. We have talked about calling our town Denmark. . . .

March 14, 1849 [pp. 58, 82]

. . . When I first came to Wisconsin, I supposed that there would be no place to sell farm products but Milwaukee, and that it would not be possible to buy necessities anywhere else as the steamships from the older states do not put in at any other lake harbors. But now I can see that this is only because the land further north [then Milwaukee] was too thinly populated to make it worthwhile for them to call there. And last summer a steamship, the Michigan, from Buffalo in New York State, called at Green Bay four times, and the propeller Rochester has sailed from Chicago to Manitowoc all summer, and there is no doubt that the shipping business will increase.

From our countrymen who came up here last summer I heard about how good the land was here. The land around Milwaukee has been sold within a distance of 50 miles, and it will always be expensive to buy the second time, so some of them had traveled up here to see the land. This moved me to . . . buy two Land Warrants. It was certainly my intention to sell the land again as the price increased along with the increase in population (how fast this is happening can be seen by the fact that 13 or 14 years ago Milwaukee, which now has 15 to 16,000 citizens, was not even started). But I was so delighted to see the land which is exactly what I had wanted. It will supply almost all life's necessities. In addition to the products that can be grown in Denmark, it will produce corn, melons and sugar and this last can be manufactured for sale until I can cultivate enough to sow seed. I do not have to buy firewood. The farmers everywhere make their own soap. Salt is not nearly so expensive as in Denmark, and coffee is at least not more expensive. The taxes are very insignificant. Vinegar and syrup can also be made from the sugar of the sugar maple. It is not so difficult to get the land ready to cultivate . . . as you do not pull up the trees but just cut them above the ground (I learned this last winter with the farmer together with other useful things, such as how to thresh). . . . After the trees are chopped into such small pieces that a pair of oxen can pull them, these are then hitched up. An iron chain is fastened around the logs, and you drag them into a heap to be burned. All this can be done by one man, and in a couple of years he can clear enough to grow what he needs to support a family, if it is not too large. . . .

You can see from my last letter that it was my plan to travel to the Mississippi River to work on a steamboat, but I got to Chicago a couple of days too late. The canal which connects the Illinois River with Lake Michigan was frozen over, so I had to either take the mail wagon or walk—and neither of these means of travel appealed to me for such a long journey. Maybe it is just as well that I did not go there as cholera has raged in New Orleans and up the Mississippi this winter. I preferred therefore to go out in the country and find work as a wheelwright. I had no more clothes with me than I could carry. I left everything else I had in

Milwaukee with a tailor Jensen from Ringsted, where my bed linens also are. I followed the canal, which is new and where I knew that everything is prospering, and the other day I reached the town of Lockport in Will County in the state of Illinois. Here I asked about work as a wheelwright which I got. I asked for 12 dollars for the first month; he offered me 10 which I took. . . .

Wilmington, Illinois, November 25, 1849 [p. 59]

. . . If you read the newspapers, you will surely know of the peace between the United States and Mexico. The latter had to give up a lot of land in, among other places, California, and shortly after they gave it up, this land was found to be richer in gold than any known land. The gold was first found in rocks and later in small nuggets in the loose top soil near the rivers which had washed it down from the mountains. . . . Not until recently have they discovered the veins where it lies. But there is so much in the ground that if a man fills a bowl with soil and holds it under the water and stirs it until the soil is rinsed away, and the gold because of its weight has collected in the bottom, he can figure on washing out a couple of lots a day. This temptation was so great that all the people left their businesses to pan gold. . . . Hundreds of ships have already sailed from Boston, New York, Philadelphia, New Orleans and other places to exchange their pork, wheat flour and clothes for gold.

Many of those I know have left to go there, and many around here that I do not know. Some of them have written home that they have already made several thousand dollars; anyone who wants to pan gold can do so, and all other work increases in price at the same rate as the profits from gold expeditions. I have written this to you because it is possible that I will accompany some of the others from this place; according to the newspapers, a good craftsman can make from 10 to 16 dollars a day, and as the gold mines . . . are said to be inexhaustible, there is no longer any fear that the daily wage will be low. You can see where California is on the map; in any case, I can tell you that if I go there, I will be many hundreds of miles further away from you than I am now. Anyway, if I go there, there is a hope that I will become rich, and if that happens, then it is possible—God willing—that I shall end my days in Denmark which I have no desire to do if I can only expect to have to work for others. But if I do get rich, then Denmark is far better than America.

July 28, 1850 [p. 83]

... Most people have only been here a few years, and as the rich are well enough off where they are, those who come here on their journey westward are usually poor when they get here. ...

Everyone who comes out here must . . . work; every person here works, but in general not so very hard. I have heard of numerous fine Europeans, the so-called gentlemen farmers, who imagine they know more about farming than others, who came over and bought land and hired people and meant to live just like at home and be in charge; but that does not work here as the one who does work also wants to make a profit from it. All the people here are nearly equal. If a master hits his apprentice or an apprentice his master: the punishment is the same for both. Also the gentleman should not say to his servant what the servant should not say to him. ...

January 1, 1851 [p. 84]

... On the evening of October 9th I came to Milwaukee where I found Mossin and his wife and little daughter. ... On the same day another Dane from Ribe arrived; he and his brother-in-law had left at the outbreak of war to avoid serving in the army and had left their wives behind. They bought land in the neighborhood of where mine is. Their house is near the road, so if countrymen who come over here wish to find our settlement, they can get directions if they take the road from Green Bay to Cooperstown. —We went with them to the settlement. We found all in good health and heard that no one had been sick since they had come there. I met an old acquaintance, Frederik Lerche; his parents and brothers and sisters had come over a couple of months ago. They had just finished their house and moved in while I was there.

I immediately began to fell trees for a house and got the frame raised, but as it would not pay for me to stay and finish . . . , I paid [Rasmus] Rasmussen to get it ready by next summer. I also arranged with Niels Godtfredsen to clear and fence about 4 to 8 acres of land for me for 12½ dollars an acre. I like the locality here even better than before. It is truly fine soil.

You will probably conclude from these preparations that I am planning to marry next summer, but that is not the case. But if I want to sell my property, then it is well worth it to make improvements on it, and if I do decide to settle down there, then it would be a big advantage to have everything ready to move in. ...

If it is too difficult for Father and Mother to stay in the house, then they should not keep it; if I do return to stay there, I hope the condition of my pocket will be such that I will not consider becoming a smallholder, and if I can do no better than that, I can assure you that I will immediately set my course for the United States of America. . . .

I am very glad I emigrated, and I should really never wish to see Denmark again if you did not live there, even though there are many of my friends I would like to speak with. . . .

October 1851 [p. 182]

. . . If Denmark should disappoint you, you need not be afraid to come over here. If Father and Mother are well, they can certainly stand the journey, as it is patience and not a lot of effort that is required, and old folk are rarely sick, but infants die for the most part . . . , but I have never heard of any who have died. You must not think that I am writing this all based only on my own experience, as I have only made the journey once. You must remember that every day I talk with people who have come over from Europe, and *all of those I meet* say the same. —I would advise young men who have only themselves to look after and no one to help them to come over here, even if they do not have much more money than it costs to cross the Ocean. But they must be prepared to take the first job they can get, even if they have to work only for board for the first month or so. They will soon find an opportunity to earn four times as much as at home. . . .

From what you hear of America, you will probably conclude that all the people here are or will be rich, but that is not the case. People seek to live well and comfortably; there are few who think of saving up for their children. If they are worth anything, they can earn their own money. The boys do not have to be bought out of military service, and the farms do not have to be leased, therefore, everyone provides for himself. . . .

August 14, 1853 [p. 84]

. . . At the present time, the railroad frenzy is greater than ever before. . . . Most of these railroads are not yet completed, and a large number of workers are required. The wages have therefore continued to increase, likewise the price of horses and cattle. . . . You have probably read in the newspapers about McCormick's reaping machine which won a prize the year before last at the World's Fair in London. . . . In London they thought it was something new. Here almost every well-to-do farmer has one. I think there are about 20 different kinds in use around here, some for cutting grass and others for reaping, and some that can be used for both. It is fast, and I have heard it said that it is impossible to do it as well with a scythe. For the most part, the machines are very simple and would not cost much more than a wagon if the inventor did not have exclusive rights to make them. As it is now, they cost about twice as much, but anyone who invents a useful and, up to now, unknown tool or machine . . . can get a patent for either seven or 14 years . . . for $30, and the inventor must swear that he believes that such a thing has not been known before. I think McCormick has made a lot of money from his reaping machine. . . . I have seen his workshop in Chicago. . . . The Patent Law encourages everyone to try to invent things, and these days almost all the things we use daily are cheaper than where you are, even though the wages here are about five times as high. . . .

A word to you, Dear Parents. You must not be angry with me because I do not return. It is a long way, and the journey costs a lot. In Denmark there is only poverty and slavery; here there is plenty and freedom. —It is not difficult for me, who has known both, to say which is best. . . .

July 15, 1855 [p. 85]

Upon arrival we found the house in ruins [the house Rasmussen had finished for him in 1851], and the clearing had not been sown. I set to work at once, and things look better already as Niels Godtfredsen immediately began to plow and sow and harrow for me, while I traveled to Manitowoc to pick up out clothes and to buy housekeeping necessities. During this time Johanne planted potatoes. It is rather late, but I hope to be able to harvest something. We have also gotten a cow which calved four weeks ago, and we have the calf, too. We are living with old school teacher Lærke until I can get a new house built for us; I have sold the old one together with all the land south of the river, so now we have only about 300 acres. . . .

November 30, 1856 [pp. 43, 85]

. . . The two farmhands from Margrethehåb wanted to accompany us to Wisconsin, and we bought tickets from New York to Manitowoc. We were 16 Danes traveling together from Copenhagen, and all were well when we reached Buffalo, but there Anders Larsen from Sorø took sick, and Lars from Margrethehåb got such terrible diarrhea that he asked me to go with him to the doctor. I did that, and Lars got a powder which helped right away. It was on the morning of the 26th of June, if I remember right. The next morning we sailed by steamship to Manitowoc. Toward evening Anders Larsen died. Lars took leave of his senses that night; he kept saying that he was about to die and gave Christen his money belt. I had already asked in the cabin next door if there was a doctor among the passengers, but there was none. Our next hope was the next landing; I knew we were near Cleveland. I asked the Captain how long he would stay there, and he said about six hours. I decided to take the chance of leaving the ship. Johanne was very unhappy as she feared the ship would sail without me, but I explained to her that it was my duty and promised to meet her in Sheboygan if the ship sailed. I would then go overland by train and get there first. We reached Cleveland in the early morning, and I immediately left the ship, but people had not yet got up, and I had to run a long distance before I found a doctor, and when I finally found one, it did not help much. He gave Lars a powder and ordered us to wash his head with cold water and bathe his feet in hot water. We did this for a few hours, but he became worse and threatened several times to jump overboard. It was one of the worse days of my life, and we felt quite sure he would die if he stayed on board as we still had three days' sailing to Manitowoc. I had to leave the ship again and after running in vain for about two hours in constant fear that the ship would sail without me, I finally found two doctors who were partners. They promised to care for him and cure him, for which I agreed to pay $45. I rented a carriage, and Christen and I accompanied him to the house where he was carried in. It was the home of a widow. He got a good room, and a man was fetched to look after him. I paid one of the doctors the 45 dollars and accepted his receipt. We left him with heavy hearts and got back to the ship in time. . . .

I promised to come if I could sell what I owned at a reasonable price. I then left and took the chest that I had left here [in Wilmington] with me, as I had little hope of selling in Wisconsin. I traveled by train to Milwaukee, and there I had to stay for three days because of a storm [on Lake Michigan]. This did not cost me anything as I have a standing invitation with Mossin, but I was eager to get home. . . . On the 4th day the weather was good, and I left on the steamship for Manitowoc. From there I joined up with one of my neighbors, a Norwegian by the name of Zacharias Johansen, who had recently sold his land, and before we reached home, I had sold him the 40 acres of land I had bought from Christian Lærche together with my goods and animals for $750. But it was on the condition that if Johanne did not want to do this, the contract was not binding.

Johanne and I talked the situation over, as, of course, it was a very important thing since we were doing well and had prospects of doing even better. We had nine head of cattle—large and small—three sheep, three pigs, and a flock of chickens and, all in all, everything we needed to live a happy life, but, on the other hand, there were many difficulties to cope with. In the beginning, Johanne could help me every time it was needed, and then it was easy to finish our work, but after she got the child to look after, of course, she could not spend so much time in the field, and when you have to hire too many people, then you might just as well cut back to what you can manage on your own. I figured that with ordinary luck we could probably save $100 a year. Those who have children can now make much more; according to what I have worked out, a boy of 12 is as good as a man you would have to hire for $1,000. But since it is not so easy to bring forth a boy of that age . . . , we decided to go to Wilmington as we thought that if we did not like it, then we could always go back. We still had the little house that I built when we arrived and 220 acres of land, and about 5 acres are cultivated.

We then left New Denmark on Tuesday, the 21st of October, and reached Manitowoc by wagon that evening. Wednesday morning at 9 o'clock we sailed for Chicago where we arrived at daybreak on Thursday. We took the first train and were in Wilmington before midday. I decided that I should take this opportunity to show Johanne some of the wonders of America, and, therefore, we took the most expensive place on the steamship, and that is something King Frederik VII in all his kingdom cannot match in splendor or in comfort. . . .

New Denmark, January 2, 1860 [p. 86]

. . . As far as I remember, I have already told you that I repurchased the 40 acres of land that I had sold when I went to Wilmington. There is a very good house on the land and about 22 acres cultivated, but this time I took it over in poor condition as [grain] had been grown on a large part of it for four years, and Zacharias Johnson continued to cultivate the oldest part of it because it was the best to plow. He was brought up underground in the silver mines of Kongsberg, and as farming is done mostly above ground, it is no wonder that he has not much understanding of it. . . .

I bought myself a couple of good oxen for 80 dollars and plowed the land as no winter plowing had been done. 3½ bushels of rye had been sown, and I had 2¾ bushels of spring wheat. The manure heap had not thawed till then, and I had seven years of manure to spread on the land where I had sown 3½ bushels of peas. Then I sowed 2¾ bushels of barley, and 4 bushels of oats. At the same time, I sowed both fields with both clover and timothy. On June 1st I sowed 3 bushels of oats on newly cleared land, and on June 20th I sowed another 3½ bushels of oats; this last I harvested green for feed.

We had a lot of nights with freezing temperatures during the summer which hurt the rye and potatoes, and the hay also suffered from it. This is the biggest plague we have, and because of the rather cold climate we have here, not many try to grow corn which, apart from this, is a profitable crop. My barley was partly eaten by worms right after it came up and was therefore thin and poor. We had a good harvest from most of what we sowed except for the last oats, they got too much rain . . . , but we finally brought that in, and the cattle are also eating it. I have winter plowed most of the land and improved everything, as much as I have been able to manage.

I will now tell you what we have gotten out of our work. First we made 80 pounds of sugar and 7 buckets of syrup and 60 pots [1 pot = approx. 1 quart] of vinegar from our maple trees. The syrup is better than the best you can buy, but the sugar is not as good as ordinary brown sugar. Then we harvested nearly 8 bushels of timothy hay. . . . We got 36 bushels of rye, 27 bushels of barley, 45 bushels of wheat, 60 bushels of potatoes, 12 bushels of carrots, 6 bushels of beets and 2 bushels of scallions. We have measured approx. 27 bushels of peas. I think that is about half of it. We are still harvesting the other crops. We have not threshed any oats yet.

Now I will tell you about our livestock. Together with the land I also bought back a cow and a calf. It was the same as I bought four years ago. . . . Early in April I bought a cow for $27.50 which had a calf six weeks ago, but I did not get that one. It is a good cow. The price of cattle has continued to fall over the past year, and in the fall I bought what I think is a good cow for $15. We therefore have six head, namely a pair of work oxen, a bull calf and a heifer . . . , and two milk cows. Shortly before the

harvest, I drove to Green Bay with 80 pounds of butter which I sold for
$10. . . . In May I bought a couple of suckling pigs from Jens Rasmussen
from Gjevninge for $1 each; we have just butchered them [at Christmas].
. . . Our stock is made up of what I have just mentioned and a dog, cats,
a good flock of chickens and a couple of ducks.

The blacksmith's son Jens from Lyndby has been staying with us
since we came up here [from Wilmington]. He works for me when I need
him, and I give him ½ dollar a day and board. When I do not need him,
he works for himself and pays me $1.25 a week for board. During the
winter he threshes my grain for every ninth *tønde* and board. There are
threshing machines here which drive around the settlement; it costs less,
but for the sake of the feed, I prefer threshing by hand. . . .

Things are better for me this winter than they have ever been before.
My work consists mostly of tending the cattle and chopping wood. . . .

February 16, 1861 [p. 88]

. . . For the past year we have had unusually good weather, and as a result of this, the harvest in Wisconsin has been especially good. I have harvested 123 bushels of wheat after using 7 bushels of seed, and 77 bushels
of rye using 3½ bushels of seed. . . . Until now the price of grain has
been low, and we may not have to take out grain to town by sled first; in
the summer the roads are bottomless mire, and you can only drive a little way at a time. Pork brings a good price, for the most part, and I have
six pigs which I think will pay well.

I told you in a previous letter that Casper and I made a trip further
inland, and I decided then to buy property there. I have since done that,
and as soon as I can sell the 40 acres where the buildings are and the land
is cultivated, we may move there. The land . . . consists of 55 acres of
heavy clay and is very flat. It borders on a small lake full of fish and wild
duck. Beside the lake I have about 6 acres of good meadow with no trees
on it; there are also 3 to 4 acres of cultivated farm land. There are three
towns just as close as you are to Roskilde; they are Neenah, Menasha and
Appleton. In the summer, steamships sail through the lake from Green
Bay to Oshkosh and other towns and out to the Fox River. And there is
a railroad which crosses my land and connects with other railroads, so
you can travel on it to all the bigger towns and all the way to New York.
I paid 825 dollars for the land. There are no buildings on it, and it is
wooded except for what I have described above. The land we live on, and

that I will sell, consists of 40 acres, about 25 acres of which are cultivated. There are very nice buildings on it, and the land is good although not quite level. —I have put it up for sale for 500 dollars. . . .

New Denmark, December 11, 1861 [p. 89]
. . . Things are still . . . about as good for us as we can ask for. Here [in New Denmark] we now have and will always have free grass for our cattle whether we have few or many. We probably will not have that for long there [in Neenah]. On the other hand, here we have nearly 4 Danish miles [approx. 18.6 U.S. miles] to the towns; there it is only half a mile. Here all the neighbors are Danish; there most are American which I prefer. . . .

Neenah, June 24, 1864 [p. 89]
. . . When I got here I found a farmhouse . . . one and a half stories without beams. We could have made do with the house, but we were used to having a cellar and could not do without. So last year I built a shed on the side with a cellar under. It is a wooden structure, and the cellar has wooden walls and a wooden floor. . . . I have built a new barn, 46 feet long and 22 feet wide. There are some young cherry trees here which bear very good cherries. I have planted 28 apple trees, six pear trees, six plum trees, and four cherry trees, I addition to some gooseberry bushes and some strawberries. The trees are grafted, and the apple trees are about 6 feet high. . . . . It is my intention to plant some every year until I have about 3 acres. Our land is well suited for grass and hay. We have 13 head of cattle, but seven are young animals, and two are work oxen. We have seven sheep of our own and seven I got from a man in Neenah who owns a piece of land next to me. . . . From them I get half of the wool and lambs. Until now Johanne has spun the wool, and we have sold the yarn. . . .

December 10, 1865 [p. 90]
. . . I have sold cattle for about $100, and furthermore, the herd is better than it was last spring. Last summer we made a good income from the sale of butter and eggs, and we plan to carry this further as soon as the children are able to help milk the cows; we live conveniently near the towns for selling everything, and it is not as difficult a job as growing grain. It is also my intention, as the tree roots rot and I can find the work-

ers, to lay drainage ditches on my land so I can grow as much grain as possible so I will no longer need to cultivate so much of it—also to make it easier to handle as my land is heavy clay, but seems to be very fertile. . . .

Our closest neighbors are Danes and Americans, but there are Germans, Frenchmen and Irish close by. Here there is still so much uncultivated land that the cattle walk where they want in the summer, but it probably will not be many years before everyone will hold on to what is his here in this area.

The price of land nearby varies from $10 to $50 per acre, but the further you get from the towns, the cheaper it is, and where there is land wonder by the government, it is always available for 1 1/4 dollars per acre, or if a family will settle immediately on it and stay for five years, they can get 160 [acres] for the cost of surveying and having the papers made up. . . . Two years ago we were the only Danish family here. There was an old bachelor from Jutland here, and he is still around. Now there are six families and four unmarried farmers who own land very close together. Wherever you come here in Wisconsin, you meet Danes. Most are poor when they come over here, but as soon as they have been here for a few years, most become prosperous. This is, because the wages are high and the land cheap.

My paper is about filled; I will therefore close with the fondest greetings to you and all my friends and acquaintances.

September 29, 1872 [p. 190]
. . . There have been no big changes here, or perhaps I should say no sudden changes, as everything certainly looks much different than it did 13 years ago when Casper and I first journeyed here by foot from New Denmark. But things have changed little by little, so you do not really notice it. Just the same, it seems to me that Johanne and I remain about the same. Perhaps I look a little older now than when you last saw us [1855]. . . . Caroline is now 16 1/2 years old and is 2 inches taller than her mother. Last February she began to take piano lessons at a convent built a couple of years ago by the Catholics, and the same nun who teaches music also has a little private school, so Caroline started to go to school regularly about six weeks ago; for this I pay 4 dollars every quarter; I pay 5 dollars for the music. —Andrew is now 14 years old and is rather big and strong for his age. He helps with the work in the summer and goes to school in the winter. . . .

Because of the high wages paid for labor, I am very careful that the children should learn everything that can benefit them in the future, and although Caroline now studies music and the sciences, which I know little about, she has first learned to cook and bake and to milk cows and use a sewing machine and has sewn her own clothes since she was 14. . . .

November 25, 1875 [p. 98]

. . . We have from time to time heard of the great progress Denmark has made in all industrial areas and that the average standard of living is much higher than when we left the country. And you write that wages are high. Here they are always complaining that wages are low. . . .

Last summer I hired a lad for 14 dollars a month; he was a bungler, and still he thought that I paid him too little. When we harvested the hay and seed grain, I paid a good laborer $1.75 a day.

This winter I have hired a young fellow for 9 dollars a month; he has just started, and I do not know yet how good he is. Last summer one of my American neighbors hired a Danish hand who was a little better than average and paid him $18.75 a month. Now he has offered him $175 for a whole year, but the fellow is demanding $225. In the country they get their board, just like with you. In the factories the workmen have to provide their own food.

Thank God we have rather good health. My son is now 17 years old; he is big and stronger than I, but he should go to school this winter, and I usually have one or more public duties that slow me down a lot; otherwise we would not have to hire hands in the winter. . . . The harvest here in Wisconsin was exceptionally fine, and our own harvest was average. Prices for most products are very good. Last winter we had the coldest day in my experience. On February 9, which was the coldest day, the Fahrenheit thermometer fell to 40 degrees below zero. This unusual cold did a lot of damage to the fruit trees, and over half of our wonderful apple trees died. Such cold is not unusual in Minnesota, but here in Wisconsin it has not been so cold since white settlers came here. . . .

There are Danes almost everywhere now, but here there is room enough for them as half of the land here in Wisconsin is not yet cultivated. . . .

July 17, 1876 [p. 99]

. . . The emigrants who come over here every year tell us, of course, how everything looks in Denmark, and from them we have heard that the wages are considerably higher than when we left, and from your letter, I can see that you now pay 2 *kroner* a day at harvest time. The consequence of this will be that, like us, the farmers in Denmark will do most of the work and the hardest work themselves with machines. From your letter I see that Frederik can now drive a couple of horses, and, basically, that is about all that is needed to use most of the machinery. I hear that you have already been using sowing machines for some time. I have only one now that sows and harrows at the same time. It sows better than can be done by hand, and harrows at the same time better than a Swedish harrow, ands the best thing of all is that a little boy or an old man can sow the seed if only they can drive a couple of horses as the driver can sit on the machine and drive it. I was one of the first here in the neighborhood to buy a mowing machine, that was about six or seven years ago, and it is still good, but most now buy machines that can both mow and reap. Horse rakes with steel teeth have been in use here for perhaps 25 years, but not until this year have I found one that I have known for a long time would come. Its most important advantage over the other types is that just by putting his foot on a wire, the driver can lift the teeth out of the hay, and as soon as he takes his foot off, it falls down and rakes again. My sowing machine (it is called Fountain City) cost $55.00. The horse rake is called Bay State Rake and costs $40.00, and I think both are about the best of their kind.

It seems to me that it would be worthwhile for you to consider whether you would be better off to buy American farming equipment which I suppose is for sale in Copenhagen. In a couple of years, with a sowing machine, a reaper-mowing machine and perhaps a horse rake, Frederik will be able to do all this kind of work with a pair of horses if you help him get started. We put the hay in the barn with a horse, but your buildings are too low for that. The posts in our barns are 18 feet high. . . .

August 2, 1888 [p. 142]

Dear Brother.

It has been so long since you have received a letter from me, and you could easily have reason to believe I had completely forgotten you. And even more time might have passed had it not been that a sad misfortune has reminded me.

My wife died on the 25th of May.

She had felt a little poorly a number of times this winter, but not more than that she always cared for the house. I did fear, however, that her weakness was in the heart and that she perhaps would die suddenly, but she continued to protest that she was not very sick.

The day she died I had been in Neenah and had just come home a little before dinner; I went in to change my clothes, and my wife had sat down at a table with a mirror in front of her and was combing her hair. We talked a little, and as I looked at her face, I saw her pale and begin to slide down between the table and the chair she was sitting on. I immediately took her in my arms and held her before she could fall, and after only a few seconds, she opened her eyes again. She looked me in the face and smiled and asked: "What was that?" I told her that she had fainted, and she answered very calmly: "Yes, I believe I did." Then right away she said: "It feels like I am going to throw up; take me outside." The weather was warm, and the door was open, so I held her tightly and led her outside, but immediately after she fainted again while I was holding her. I called to my son who was close by, and we carried her in and placed her on the bed, but all attempts to bring her back to life failed, and my son then ran to Neenah as quickly as he could, and called a doctor who came an hour and a half after my wife had fainted, but he told us that she was dead.

My wife's death is the only great sorrow that has befallen us up to now, and we feel it very strongly. None of the children are married, and we all live together and are, incidentally, fine. We have a hired man and a hired girl, both Danish.

I do not know whether you have any interest in my telling you how we do our business. I continue to buy a little more land when a piece I like is up for sale, so I now own about 170 acres, and it is worth from 70 to 75 dollars an acre. About half of it has never been cultivated. We have concentrated most on animal breeding, especially horses, and at the present time we have 16. We have 24 head of cattle and 40 sheep. That includes both young and old, but the number varies considerably from time to time; we have recently sold seven two-year old steers, and that is the age at which we prefer to sell horses and cattle. In recent years we have kept a half-bred Clydesdale stallion, but this year we sold it, and at present we have none. We have fine foals, and we have bred seven mares. Our horses are, by the way, all mares, except for colts and foals. Our cattle are shorthorn Durham, and we have a thoroughbred bull of that breed. The sheep are mixtures of the Cotswold breed, but we have a thoroughbred Shropshire Down ram.

Casper [his traveling companion from 1847] came to visit me recently. Except for the fact that he suffers from kidney stones, he is well for his age. He lives in New Denmark as always and is rich. I have not heard from you for a long time, and ask that you write and tell me how you are—how many children you have—how old they are and how they are doing. —

Give my greetings to all old friends and acquaintances.

My wife's death reminds me that our time will soon be up, and I will bid you farewell and wish you God's Peace and Blessing.

Your brother, Andrew Frederickson

BIBLIOGRAPHY AND FURTHER READING

Bille, John H. "A History of the Danes in America," *Transactions of the Wisconsin Academy of Sciences, Arts and Letters*, 11 (March 1896), 1–48.

Christensen, Thomas P. "Danish Settlement in Wisconsin," *Wisconsin Magazine of History*, 12 (1928), 19–40.

Danish Baptist General Conference of America. *Seventy-Five Years of Danish Baptist Missionary Work in America* (Philadelphia: American Baptist Publication Society, 1932).

Hale, Frederick, "The Americanization of a Danish Immigrant in Wisconsin, 1847–1872," *Wisconsin Magazine of History*, 64 (1980–1981), 202–215.

Hansen, Thorvald. *School in the Woods: The Story of an Immigrant Seminary* (Askov, Minnesota: American Publishing Company, 1977).

Hvidt, Kristian. *Flight to America: The Social Background of 300,000 Danish Emigrants* (New York: Academic Press, 1975).

Jensen, John M. *The United Evangelical Lutheran Church: An Interpretation* (Minneapolis: Augsburg Publishing House, 1964).

Jeppesen, Torben Grøngaard. *Dannebrog on the American Prairie: A Danish Colony Project in the 1870s: Land Purchase and the Beginnings of a Town* (Odense, Denmark: Odense City Museums, 2000).

Marzolf, Marion. *The Danish-language Press in America* (New York: Arno Press, 1979).

Mortensen, Enok. *The Danish Lutheran Church in America: The History and Heritage of the American Evangelical Lutheran Church* (Philadelphia: Fortress Press, 1967).

Mortensen, Enok. *Schools for Life: Grundtvigian Folk Schools in America* (Junction City, Oregon: Danish American Heritage Society, 1977).

Nyholm, Paul C. *The Americanization of the Danish Lutheran Churches in America* (Copenhagen: Kirkehistoriske Studier, 1963).

Stilling, Niels Peter and Anne Lisbeth Olsen. *A New Life: Danish Emigration to North America as Described by the Emigrants Themselves in Letters, 1842–1946* (Aalborg, Denmark: Danes Worldwide Archives in collaboration with the Danish Society for Emigration History, 1994).

THE AUTHOR

FREDERICK HALE (born 1948) graduated from Macalester College in 1969 and was awarded master's degrees at Harvard University, the University of Minnesota, and the Johns Hopkins University. He received his Doctor of Philosophy at Johns Hopkins in 1976. In addition to *Danes in Wisconsin* he has written five books in the field of Scandinavian immigration and has contributed articles to historical, literary, and theological journals in the United Kingdom, Scandinavia, Africa, and the United States.

INDEX

Referencs to photos are in italic type